Ready? Click!

by Caren B. Stelson

illustrated by Sandra Shap

MODERN CURRICULUM PRESS
Pearson Learning Group

Pack your bags.
Take your camera.
Jump in the truck.
And we are off!

What will you see?
You will see animals you will
never forget.

Look! There is an elephant!
What do you know about
elephants?

Did you know this?
Elephants like to take
baths—dirt baths!

How about a picture?
Get out your camera.
Ready? Click!

Look! There is a giraffe!
What do you know about giraffes?

Did you know this?
A giraffe's tongue is very long—
about as long as your arm.

How about a picture?
Ready? Click!

What luck! There's a rhino.
What do you know about rhinos?

Did you know this?
Rhinos have three toes on
each foot.

How about a picture?
Ready? Click!

Shhhhh. Lions! Can you see them in that patch of grass? What do you know about lions?

Did you know this? Lions sleep a lot—up to twenty hours a day!

How about a picture?
Get out your camera.
Ready? Click!

Look over there in the river.
They are not rocks in the mud.
They are hippos.
Hippos must stay out of the sun.
Their skin gets sunburned fast!

How about a picture?
Ready? Click!

Look at the zebras.
Do you know why zebras
have stripes?

Some people think stripes help zebras tell one friend from another.

What do you think?

There is time for one more picture.
Ready? Click!
I can not wait until our next trip!